DOG

Brian David Walker

BROADWAY PLAY PUBLISHING INC
New York
www.broadwayplaypublishing.com
info@broadwayplaypublishing.com

DOG
© Copyright 2021 Brian David Walker

Cover painting: *A Pomeranian* by Antoine Dury, 1888

First edition: October 2021
I S B N: 978-0-88145-912-8

Book design: Marie Donovan
Page make-up: Adobe InDesign
Typeface: Palatino

ACKNOWLEDGMENTS

This play wouldn't be what it is today without the feedback and insight of several fantastic theatre artists along its journey to publication. First, I'd like to thank Kathi E B Ellis who directed the first reading of the play, and the cast and production team at the Kentucky Theatre Association's annual conference in 2013. Second, Jonathan Williams and the cast and production team of the 2014 reading at Capital Stage's Playwright Revolution. Third, I'd like to thank Jeffrey K Miller and the cast and production team at Cincinnati Lab Theatre for the October 2020 online production. Finally, I will be forever grateful to Christopher Gould, Michael Q Fellmeth and everyone at Broadway Play Publishing Inc for their guidance, grace and belief in my play.

CHARACTERS & SETTING

BAILEY, 34, *female, owned a dog but it ran away, eccentric*

JOAN, 41, *female, owns a dog and is wife to* PHIL, *passive*

PHIL, 44, *male, owns a dog and is husband to* JOAN, *aggressive*

BEN, 31, *male, brother to* JOAN, *stoner (artist stoner not hippie stoner)*

Time, place: Now. Louisville, Kentucky. A café, JOAN *and* PHIL's *upper-middle class home, a sidewalk, a dog park.*

*This play may be performed without an intermission. If an intermission is preferred, it should go between Scene 3 and 4.

"Heaven goes by favor. If it went by merit, you would stay out and your dog would go in."
—Mark Twain

"Dogs love their friends and bite their enemies, quite unlike people, who are incapable of pure love and always have to mix love and hate."
—Sigmund Freud

"I've seen a look in dogs' eyes, a quickly vanishing look of amazed contempt, and I am convinced that basically dogs think humans are nuts."
—John Steinbeck

Dedicated to Rosie, the best dog I ever knew

Scene 1

(*Lights up on a coffee shop.* BAILEY *sits across from* JOAN *and* PHIL. *They all stare at each other uncomfortably for several moments.*)

PHIL: I guess I'll start. What do you want?

BAILEY: I want to talk.

PHIL: You're lucky we've even decided to meet with you.

BAILEY: I'm sorry.

JOAN: Don't start that way—

PHIL: I'll start any damned way I feel like starting, she wasn't saying anything.

BAILEY: I know that this is complicated but I did want to just start by apologizing to you.

PHIL: That'd be a great place to start.

(*They stare at each other for a moment.*)

PHIL: Well?

BAILEY: What?

PHIL: Was that it? Was that the apology?

BAILEY: I'm sorry?

JOAN: No, I think that was it.

PHIL: Which was it?

BAILEY: Which was what?

PHIL: You said you wanted to start by apologizing to us but I'm still waiting for a sufficient version of that apology.

BAILEY: *(Apologizing)* I'm sorry.

(They stare at each other for a few moments.)

PHIL: Fine.

JOAN: Well, we accept your apology. We understand?

PHIL: We do?

JOAN: Phil—

PHIL: Don't lie to the woman, alright? Look, we don't understand. We accept your apology but my wife is being premature in saying we understand, you understand?

BAILEY: Yes, I'm sorry.

PHIL: Alright, alright, that's enough, I get the point.

BAILEY: Okay. I don't even really remember what happened, it was all so fast. I'm sorry.

They stare at each other for a few moments.

PHIL: You acted like a crazy person—

BAILEY: I know I must've—

PHIL: You shouldn't do that, you never know about people, had we been some of those gun toting assholes you may have—

JOAN: Don't say that to her—

PHIL: You should think about those things before you go crazy on a complete stranger, that's all I'm saying. The city park isn't for confrontation.

BAILEY: You're right.

PHIL *(To* JOAN*)* See, she agrees with me.

BAILEY: I wasn't thinking, honestly I've never done anything like that before. I was just so…overtaken… with…emotion—

JOAN: We understand.

PHIL: Stop saying that!

BAILEY: I saw him and I couldn't-I just-I love him so much— If you were in my position—

PHIL: I certainly wouldn't have—

JOAN: The thing is, we love him very, very much.

BAILEY: So do I.

PHIL: Look, what do you want?

BAILEY: I want my dog back.

PHIL: Here we go—

JOAN: But we love him—

PHIL: How do you even know it's your dog, that's what I don't understand, all dogs look the same, how do you even—

BAILEY: I know it's him—

JOAN: When did you say you lost him again?

BAILEY: Last year.

JOAN: What month?

BAILEY: July.

JOAN: Oh.

BAILEY: When did you adopt him?

PHIL: Don't answer that—

BAILEY: Why not?

PHIL: Look, we don't owe you anything, alright, the only reason we're even here is to give you this—

(PHIL *takes out a piece of paper and hands it to* BAILEY.)

BAILEY: What's this?

PHIL: An invoice.

BAILEY: An invoice?

PHIL: When you pushed my wife into the pond, you do remember doing that, don't you?

BAILEY: I'm sorry—

PHIL: When you pushed my wife into the pond she was wearing a very expensive watch and now it doesn't work anymore.

JOAN: We're just asking that you fix it, not replace it, that's what the invoice is for, it isn't beyond repair and I was just wearing some old shorts so I'm not worried about those but the watch was-special-it was supposed to mean something—

BAILEY: I'm sorry I did that. I really am.

PHIL: Our mailing address is on the bottom there, you can just send the check there please.

BAILEY: Six hundred dollars?

PHIL: It was a very expensive watch—

JOAN: If you need to send it in small chunks, that's fine—

PHIL: *(Standing)* Let's go, Joan *(He stands.)* we gave it to her, we've got to get moving—

BAILEY: No, no, wait, I'm not done talking to you about this yet.

PHIL: We're going to be late if we don't—

BAILEY *(Screaming at the top of her lungs)* I'M NOT DONE TALKING TO YOU ABOUT MY DOG YET!

(They stare at each other for a few moments. PHIL sits back down.)

PHIL: Fine. Talk.

BAILEY: Rosie.

PHIL: Rosie?

BAILEY: My dog's name is Rosie.

JOAN: Our dog's name is Duke. He's responded to it since the day we got him.

PHIL: It was the name they gave him at the shelter—

BAILEY: Duke?

PHIL: What kind of name is Rosie for a boy dog anyway?

BAILEY: It was because of his coat—

PHIL: A male dog needs a masculine name—

BAILEY: The color of his coat—

JOAN: He's responded to Duke since the day we got him.

BAILEY: I just-I'm sorry-Duke?

PHIL: We've got to leave.

BAILEY: I want Rosie back.

JOAN: Duke's our dog now.

BAILEY: But I lost him—

PHIL: We don't even know if it's your dog or not! Isn't there even a remote possibility that our Duke just looks like your Rosie?

BAILEY: It's him, I know it's him. I looked into his eyes—

PHIL: But here's the thing, even if it is him, in some parallel-crazy person-universe, he's still our dog. We adopted him.

JOAN: He really is so happy with us—

BAILEY: I don't care—

PHIL: We have the papers, we paid the money, we got his shots and had him groomed and he became our dog. And really, if he was your dog, why didn't you find him?

BAILEY: I looked everywhere! You don't know what I went through- What shelter did you adopt him from?

PHIL: I don't have to tell you anything.

JOAN: It was in Henry County, where his parents live—

PHIL: Don't tell her that!

JOAN: I don't see what the harm in telling her where your parents live—

PHIL: That's enough please—

BAILEY: (*More to herself*) How did he get all the way out to Henry County?

PHIL: Maybe, just maybe, he's not your dog!

BAILEY: But I know it.

PHIL: I don't see how.

BAILEY: There must be something I can do. I will pay you whatever you want!

PHIL: It's not about the money, he's our dog.

BAILEY: He was mine first—

PHIL: It doesn't matter, he's ours now. He didn't want to be with you, did you think of that?

(BAILEY *is completely shocked and speechless.*)

JOAN: That wasn't very nice.

PHIL: I'm starting to feel not very nice about this whole thing. We're leaving.

(PHIL *stands to leave,* JOAN *follows.*)

BAILEY: I'm going to get my dog back.

PHIL: Are you threatening us?

BAILEY: No, I'm not, I just—

PHIL: You have no idea who you're messing with, okay, I'll have my lawyer on you so quick—

JOAN: He won't, he's just saying that—

PHIL: I will so!

JOAN: We don't even have a lawyer!

PHIL: Don't tell her that!

JOAN: I'm sorry, maybe, you know, maybe you should just go adopt another dog. The shelter has so many, I mean there's so much love that needs to be spread, you know what I mean?

PHIL: I'm going to pull the car around. *(He exits.)*

BAILEY: Please. I've missed Rosie so much. He was my best friend. *(She begins crying hysterically.)*

JOAN: Oh, no, no, don't cry— *(She sits back down.)*

BAILEY: I just—I just—I thought he was dead—I thought I'd never get to see him again-

JOAN: You have to, well with animals you have to—

BAILEY: I never got to say goodbye. He was gone. He was just/gone.

JOAN: I know. I'm sorry.

BAILEY: If I could just, I mean if I was able to say that to him…

JOAN: Say what?

BAILEY: Say goodbye.

JOAN: Oh.

BAILEY: It would help me so much.

JOAN: Oh.

BAILEY: You know?

JOAN: Yes.

BAILEY: But I guess that's impossible now—

JOAN: Well—

BAILEY: Just impossible, right? Just completely impossible for me to see my dog one last time to say goodbye—

JOAN: Do you really think that would help? Wouldn't it just—

BAILEY: Yes. It would help. A lot.

JOAN: I just don't think Phil would go for it.

BAILEY: I need closure. Everyone needs closure. Have you ever just needed closure to something before?

JOAN: Of course I have.

BAILEY: So you can understand where I'm coming from—

JOAN: I can understand that.

BAILEY: *(Crying again)* I never got to say goodbye—

JOAN: Alright. Listen. Don't cry—

BAILEY: I just want to say goodbye to Rosie!

JOAN: Alright. Okay. Why don't you come over to our house? You can see him and say goodbye.

BAILEY: You'd let me do that?

JOAN: Phil is going to kill me.

BAILEY: If you do this for me, I promise, that'll be it.

JOAN: I'm trusting you not to do anything…crazy.

BAILEY: I promise—

JOAN: I understand what you're going through but you've got to be able to see it from our perspective too—

BAILEY: I'll try.

JOAN: Come have dinner with us and you'll feel better about it.

BAILEY: Dinner?

JOAN: Does that sound okay?

BAILEY: Thank you.

JOAN: Just do bring some money to put towards the watch or my husband won't be very happy.

BAILEY: I don't have six hundred dollars—

JOAN: Just bring something. I know Phil seems like a hard man but he's really a puppy dog—

(There is a loud car horn.)

BAILEY: I'll bring something.

JOAN: Okay. Well. Friday night? Let's say Seven? Does that work for you?

BAILEY: Perfect.

JOAN: *(Indicating the invoice)* You have our address there?

BAILEY: Yes.

JOAN: We'll see you Friday.

BAILEY: Thank you.

JOAN: I hate this whole thing.

BAILEY: Thank you.

JOAN exits.

BAILEY: *(Screaming at unseen customers)* WHAT ARE YOU STARING AT?

(Lights fade to black. A single dog bark is heard in the dark.)

Scene 2

(*Lights on* PHIL *and* JOAN's *place. She enters. She lights a candle on the table, which is set for dinner with four places. There is a knock on the door. She goes to the door and opens it.* BEN *stands on the other side with a bottle of wine.*)

JOAN: You're early.

BEN: I'm sorry.

JOAN: Just sit. I still have things to do.

BEN: You don't have to entertain me or anything. (*Indicating wine*) Do you already have something open or should I?

JOAN: Shouldn't we wait for everyone?

BEN: You haven't started drinking?

JOAN: I had a glass, I needed wine for the Brussels sprouts-it's on the counter still-

BEN: I'll put this in the fridge.

(BEN *exits to the kitchen.* JOAN *continues to fuss over stuff on the table. He re-enters with a glass of wine and has a seat on the couch.*)

JOAN: I'm glad you were free—

BEN: Me too. When do you guys leave for your cruise?

JOAN: Monday. Are you going to just stay here like I asked?

BEN: Duke likes it just fine at my place, it'll be fine.

JOAN: Your apartment is so small; you'd have all this space, plus the yard. Just stay here, why don't you?

BEN: I'll think about it.

JOAN: And you can help yourself to whatever you want, plus we've got the satellite and you can watch—

BEN: I said I'll think about it.

JOAN: Good, thank you.

BEN: Are you looking forward to the trip?

JOAN: I am.

BEN: It'll be good for you and Phil to just get out of the city and away from everything.

JOAN: Yes it will.

BEN: How are things going?

JOAN: Fine, things are going just fine, thank you for asking.

BEN: Yeah?

JOAN: Yes! Really, things are good right now, we're looking forward to getting on that cruise boat and just being together, so things are good.

BEN: Good because I like Phil.

JOAN: Good because you should, our relationship doesn't have anything to do with you.

BEN: I'm just saying.

JOAN: I know, I appreciate it, I really do.

BEN: If he pulls that crap again I'll kick his ass.

JOAN: You would not, he'd kill you—

BEN: I may have to pay someone else to do it but it'll happen.

JOAN: It's not going to happen again but I appreciate you always wanting to protect me. Always taking up for your big sister.

BEN: Or I'll get out my baseball bat!

JOAN: Oh God. Hank Garrett. God.

BEN: Yeah, that guy was lucky, talk about a douchebag.

JOAN: You come running out on the front porch screaming and yelling at him swinging that bat, in your pajamas—

BEN: He ran up out of there so fast—

JOAN: He was a douchebag.

(BEN *and* JOAN *share an honest laugh.*)

BEN: *(Sees the fourth place setting)* Who's the fourth?

JOAN: Oh, just this woman that I met—

BEN: A woman?

JOAN: That I met the other day—

BEN: Who is she?

JOAN: I don't really know much about her to be honest with you. Her name is Bailey. Isn't that an interesting first name? I've heard it as a last name but I don't think I've—

BEN: Is this a set-up? Please tell me you're not—

JOAN: No, no, not at all, I needed an even number and since you're perpetually at home I just thought—

BEN: Unbelievable.

JOAN: She's very nice—

BEN: You said you didn't even know her—

JOAN: I don't.

BEN: Look I don't need to be set up with strangers by my big sister, alright? I told you the last time not to do that to me again. I mean come on! This is embarrassing- you never listen to a single fucking thing I say!

JOAN: Oh don't start freaking out, alright, it's just dinner, that's it, I just needed an even number of people and I thought you and Phil could hang out.

BEN: Yeah right.

JOAN: Honest, plus we haven't seen you in weeks.

BEN: It's not the end of the world—

JOAN: I miss you. Now stop acting like an ass, this'll be nice.

(JOAN *gives* BEN *a huge hug.*)

BEN: I'm fine.

JOAN: Did you bring it?

BEN: Of course.

JOAN: Great. This'll be great then.

BEN: Who is she?

JOAN: She's the woman who pushed me into the pond at the park last week.

BEN: What? The dog woman? Are you nuts? Why?

JOAN: I just, well I don't know. I guess that I…feel bad. She really thinks that Duke is her dog—

BEN: But what if he is? What if she tries to take him again?

JOAN: No, no, that's not going to happen.

BEN: But what if she does?

JOAN: She said that she needed to say goodbye to him and I felt bad for her. I believed her. I feel connected to her for some reason. It's stupid, I know. Whether or not he is her dog I thought this could give her some closure—

BEN: Why do you care, you don't even know her?

JOAN: She's lonely. She's by herself.

BEN: And you connected?

JOAN: That's right.

BEN: And why am I here again?

JOAN: I told you, I needed even numbers. Plus—Phil.

BEN: Oh, you need me to get Phil stoned so he doesn't freak out?

JOAN: Something like that.

BEN: Exactly like that.

JOAN: Thank you for coming! This is going to be fun, we never have dinner! This is going to be fun!

BEN: I'm going to need more wine.

JOAN: We have plenty.

BEN: *(Finishing glass)* This one is good!

JOAN: Just be nice to her. She's very cute, really, you've done worse—

BEN: Unbelievable. You are just blowing me away right now!

JOAN: What?

BEN: This isn't a setup but she's very cute, very nice? Pick a lane! You're setting me up!

JOAN: This isn't a set up, I've already told you that.

BEN: Right.

JOAN: But what if you do like her, I mean that wouldn't be the worst thing in the world, would it? Life happens all the time, Ben.

BEN: I've noticed.

(PHIL enters through the front door.)

JOAN: Hi honey.

PHIL: Hey, hey Ben, what are you doing here?

BEN: Dinner.

JOAN: How was work?

PHIL: It was fine. You didn't tell me we had dinner plans.

JOAN: I didn't? I'm sorry, I could have sworn- Ben brought pot.

(PHIL *howls like a dog in excitement.*)

BEN: You wanna smoke?

PHIL: Hell yeah! What are we waiting for?

JOAN: Just go back into the bedroom, don't smoke it out here. Dinner will be ready in about twenty.

(BEN *rises to follow* PHIL *out.*)

PHIL: What a great surprise, come on. You got any bites on the comic book yet—

BEN: No, not yet, but I have another meeting on Tuesday—

JOAN: You didn't tell me that!

BEN: You didn't ask.

JOAN: That's great! Is it an interview?

BEN: Yeah, I mean I guess, I'm bringing them my book.

JOAN: It's time you got back into the workforce.

BEN: No shit.

JOAN: Go smoke, dinner will be ready soon.

They exit to the bedroom. JOAN goes to the back door.

JOAN: Duke! Come on back up here! Good boy, that's a good boy!

(JOAN *begins moving things from the kitchen to the table. The doorbell rings. She goes to open the door.* BAILEY *stands on the other side with a bottle of wine and a large duffle bag.*)

JOAN: Come in! So glad you could make it!

BAILEY: Thank you for having me. I brought wine.

JOAN: Excellent. I have a white open, would you like a glass?

BAILEY: Sure.

JOAN: Great. Be right back.

(JOAN *exits to the kitchen.* BAILEY *looks around intently. Is that weed she smells?* JOAN *re-enters with She has a glass of wine for* BAILEY *and a fresh bottle she places on the table.*)

JOAN: Can I take your bag?

BAILEY: That's okay. I'll hold onto it.

JOAN: Alright.

BAILEY: You have a lovely home.

JOAN: Thank you. So-you're sure I can't take your bag?

BAILEY: I'm sure.

JOAN: What's in it, if you don't mind me asking? It's big.

BAILEY: I know, I'm sorry, I'm such a loser, I just, it's just some stuff for Rosie—for…Duke, I wanted him to have them. *(She squeezes the bag and it squeaks.)*

JOAN: Did you want to see him?

BAILEY: *(Quickly)* No, not yet. Where is he?

JOAN: Out in the backyard. When there are squirrels—

BAILEY: Oh, I know.

JOAN: You can go back there if you want to—

BAILEY: No. I'm not ready yet.

JOAN: Oh. Okay.

BAILEY: I mean, I just want to relax for a moment, have a glass of wine-mmm, this is good.

JOAN: It's a Grigio—

BAILEY: I really like it.

JOAN: Are you sure?

BAILEY: Yes. Thank you for having me over.

JOAN: It's nothing at all-my brother stopped in so I've invited him to eat with us. I hope that's alright?

BAILEY: Of course.

JOAN: Good. His name is Ben.

BAILEY: Oh, okay.

(There is a moment of silence.)

JOAN: Do you like Brussels sprouts?

BAILEY: Yes, I do.

JOAN: And chicken?

BAILEY: Sure!

JOAN: Stupid question, I guess everyone likes chicken, don't they?

BAILEY: Not vegetarians—

JOAN: Are you a vegetarian?

BAILEY: Oh, no, no, not me. I like chicken, I was just saying, you know?

JOAN: Oh good.

BAILEY: And here's this—

(BAILEY takes a twenty dollar bill from her pocket and hands it to JOAN.)

JOAN: What's this?

BAILEY: Towards the watch.

JOAN: Oh, the watch, yes, of course. I'll give it to Phil.

BAILEY: I know it's just twenty bucks but it's all I have right now.

JOAN: No, that's fine, I appreciate the attempt, I really do, I'm sorry—

BAILEY: It's my fault. I shouldn't have pushed you into the pond.

JOAN: You are right about that!

(JOAN *attempts an awkward laugh, there is a moment of silence.*)

BAILEY: It must be a really nice watch—

JOAN: It is. I'd show it to you but we have it at the watch shop. They're waiting on a part.

BAILEY: I believe you. It's not like I think you're lying or trying to embezzle money from me because of what happened—

JOAN: You don't think that, do you?

BAILEY: I just never heard of a six hundred dollar bill to fix a watch—

JOAN: You have the invoice from the shop, call them yourself if you want to.

BAILEY: I don't want to. I was just saying.

JOAN: It was very expensive. Phil gave it to me, he was trying to get out of the doghouse, it was engraved and had, well, it has significance; it's not just the money, which is why I have to have it fixed. It's brand new/I mean he just gave it to me less than a year ago—

BAILEY: I can only imagine. What'd he do?

JOAN: (*Ignoring the question*) I hate the whole thing, I really do—

(BEN *and* PHIL *enter laughing.* PHIL *stops suddenly when he notices* BAILEY.)

PHIL: What the fuck are you doing here?

(BAILEY, *deer in headlights*)

JOAN: She's here for dinner.

PHIL: Dinner? You're kidding.

JOAN: I'm not.

PHIL: I'm not having dinner with this crazy person. I'd appreciate it if you'd leave.

BAILEY: Leave?

JOAN: She's not going anywhere. She wants to say goodbye to the dog—

BAILEY: My dog—

PHIL: We don't know that for sure—

BAILEY: I know it for sure.

PHIL: So go out there and say goodbye. Why did you have to invite her to dinner?

JOAN: Here.

(JOAN *hands* PHIL *the twenty dollar bill.*)

PHIL: What's this?

JOAN: She brought it, to go towards my watch.

PHIL: You got a long way to go. You going to cook her dinner for every twenty dollar bill?

BEN: Hi, I'm Ben.

BAILEY: Hi. Bailey.

(*They all stare at each other uncomfortably for a few moments.*)

JOAN: Can we just eat, please, have a nice meal before she says goodbye?

PHIL: I'm not comfortable with this at all and you knew I wouldn't be, this whole thing, your brother, what are you up to?

JOAN: I'm not up to anything!

BAILEY: It smells like weed.

PHIL: Mind your own business.

BAILEY: That's fine. I'll leave. Marijuana is illegal in this state you know.

PHIL: Are you threatening me?

BAILEY: Maybe. You're being rude. Your wife has cooked this lovely meal—

PHIL: Don't you dare talk to me about my wife—

BAILEY: It's just rude, that's all.

PHIL: I'm being rude? You are a crazy woman who pushed my wife into a mucky, dirty pond and I'm being rude? You have some nerve—

BAILEY: Fine, I'm leaving.

PHIL: Fine.

JOAN: No!

BAILEY: And I'll just call in my anonymous tip to the drug hotline on my way home.

PHIL: What are you talking about a drug hotline, there's no such thing.

BAILEY: Fine. Goodbye then. *(She doesn't move. She waits and stares at them.)*

JOAN: She's right, you are being rude. We're going to have dinner, a dinner that I cooked, I shopped for. If you're not hungry go in the other room.

PHIL: You threaten me again, you're out, you understand?

BAILEY: Yes.

JOAN: No one is threatening anyone, now, okay, have some wine.

PHIL: I want beer.

JOAN: Alright.

(JOAN *exits to the kitchen to get a beer.* PHIL *stares at* BAILEY *as she swigs the rest of her wine.* BEN *is amused.* JOAN *re-enters. She hands the beer to* PHIL.)

JOAN: Okay?

PHIL: Let's eat. You and I will talk when all this is over.

JOAN: Great! Try and be a good host until then if you could, okay?

PHIL: I will if you will.

BEN: *(To* BAILEY*)* So, what do you do?

BAILEY: Me, oh, you know. Stuff.

(They all stare at her uncomfortably as the lights fade to black. The sound of a dog barking several times is heard in the dark.)

Scene 3

*(*PHIL, JOAN, BAILEY *and* BEN *are finished eating. Two bottles of wine sit empty on the table.* BEN *is uncorking a third as lights come up.)*

BEN: And I was just like waiting, you know, for a really, really long time so I went up to the little like kiosk-desk thing and of course the attendant pretended to be busy on her computer screen until she finally looked up and didn't even say anything, you know those curt little customer service bitches that can't even say "can I help you?" they just look at you and give you this look, you know? So I said, how much longer are we going to have to wait and she says "when we know something you'll know something." To which I asked her if she could just approximate for me and she says "ask Obama to approximate for you, it's his fault." I was just so like mortified that this bitch—

JOAN: Please stop calling her a bitch.

BEN: What? She was a bitch! I couldn't believe she said that to me!

JOAN: We're at dinner, okay?

BEN: Okay. Who wants more wine?

BAILEY: *(Holding up her glass)* Me!

(BEN *refills glasses.)*

BEN: Who brought this one, was this yours?

BAILEY: I brought it.

BEN: I've never had it. I like the funny goose.

BAILEY: It's my go to ten dollar bottle.

BEN tries the wine.

BEN: It's really good.

BAILEY: Yeah, for ten bucks, you know? I mean, I really like it.

BEN: Me too.

PHIL: Babe, I need another beer, do you mind?

JOAN: Anyone else need anything?

(No one does. JOAN exits to the kitchen.)

BEN: So anyway I waited six and a half hours.

PHIL: Shit!

BEN: It was unbelievable.

PHIL: I hate airports.

(JOAN re-enters from the kitchen with a beer.)

JOAN: Here you are dear.

PHIL: Thanks.

BEN: I never want to spend that long in an airport again ever; they're like little cities with their own rules and social ladders—

JOAN: Social ladders?

BEN: You know what I mean and the fucking security guards! I swear to Christ they walk around acting like fucking James Garner in Gunsmoke.

BAILEY: I don't think James Garner was in Gunsmoke.

PHIL: She's right, that was James Arness.

JOAN: I don't get what you mean by social ladders—

BEN: Right, right, fucking James Arness!

JOAN: What is a social ladder anyway?

BEN: It's something you have to climb with a smile to get what you want.

JOAN: And you did that at the airport?

BEN: Fuck yeah I did! From the ticket counter to the security to the fucking gate, if you're not smiling you're suspect and they can knock you off the ladder whenever they fucking want!

JOAN: Can you please with the language?

BEN: What?

JOAN: We have a guest. That's no way to—

BEN: What's the problem?

JOAN: It's just so—

BEN: (To BAILEY) I always cuss! Do you care that I cuss?

BAILEY: I don't care, it doesn't bother me.

BEN: See, it doesn't bother her. I've been drinking. I cuss. That's what I do.

JOAN: Well it's bothering me—

BEN: Well *fuck* me.

(There is a moment of silence. PHIL begins snickering and trying not to laugh like people do when they're high and think they're not being obvious. It spreads to BEN and soon they're both in stitches.)

JOAN: What's so funny?

BEN: You.

JOAN: Great, I'm so glad I can amuse you. I'm sorry—

BAILEY: No, it's fine, I'm fine.

BEN: See, she's fine. Lighten up.

JOAN: Please don't tell me to lighten up.

BEN: Fine. Chill out.

They both begin snickering again.

JOAN: You know what— *(She stops herself.)*

BEN: What? What's what?

JOAN: Forget it.

BEN: No, you got something to say just say it.

JOAN: I changed my mind.

BEN: You're the one who asked me to come over and get him stoned—

PHIL: *(Indicating* BAILEY*)* Shhh…marijuana is illegal in this state…

(They begin snickering again.)

JOAN: Okay, I see this evening is just going to continue to digress…so who wants dessert?

BEN: You're also the one who brought me here and tried to set me up with someone—

BAILEY: What?

JOAN: This was not a setup! I wanted to have an even number!

BEN: Oh that's such bullshit and you know it! STOP TRYING TO HOOK ME UP! You're my fucking sister and it's embarrassing!

PHIL: Alright now, let's cool it—

BAILEY: I'm not here for a set-up—

JOAN: No, I know, he's reaching, that's not what this is.

BEN: Why do you even care so much if I'm by myself or not? You act like I'm crippled or something.

JOAN: I do not! There's nothing wrong with me being concerned about you being alone—

BEN: I like being alone!

JOAN: I'm just trying to help—

BEN: I don't need your help so butt out, work on your own marriage if you need a—

JOAN: JUST BECAUSE YOU GOT YOUR BALL CUT OUT DOESN'T GIVE YOU THE RIGHT TO BE AN ASSHOLE!

(There is a moment of silence.)

BEN: Fine.

(BAILEY pours herself out another full glass and begins drinking it.)

JOAN: I'll get the dessert.

JOAN exits to the kitchen.

PHIL: You guys just need to cool it, you know what assholes you both turn into with each other. Shut it down or I'm gonna have to hear about it all weekend and that's not how I intend on spending my weekend so come on—

BEN: She just gets so…infuriating!

PHIL: Hey, you're preaching to the choir here, I'm just saying, she's your sister, you need to—

(BAILEY finishes her glass and accidently slams it down on the table.)

BAILEY: Sorry. I didn't mean to do that. *(She pauses.)* Is it alright if I go see my dog now? The reason I'm here. To say goodbye.

PHIL: Hold on a minute. Let me finish what I was saying, if you don't mind?

BAILEY: I'm sorry.

PHIL: *(To* BEN*)* Be nice before you both go too far, okay?

BEN: Okay.

PHIL: *(To* BAILEY*)* Now. You. I want to ask you a question, if that's alright, you know what Gunsmoke is so you can't be all bad—

BAILEY: I used to watch Gunsmoke every night with my grandma before she passed away.

PHIL: See, that's nice. That's a nice thing to do, sit with your dying grandmother and watch an old western T V show. Most people wouldn't do something like.

BAILEY: I don't know about that.

PHIL: I know I wouldn't have the patience for it.

*(*JOAN *re-enters with four lovely trifle bowls and hands them out.)*

JOAN: Dessert!

PHIL: You seem like a good person. Like you got a good head on your shoulders.

BAILEY: I do. Is that the question?

PHIL: I just want to know: why did you act like that? Why did you push my wife in the pond and try and run off with my dog?

BAILEY: He's my dog.

PHIL: And that gives you the right to do what you did?

BAILEY: That's not what I'm saying. Something/ happened in my head-I don't know.

PHIL: Yes you do and I think I deserve to hear it, you're sitting here in my house eating my food. What happened in your head? Tell me.

BAILEY: You don't want to hear it.

PHIL: I do. I want to hear it. Honest.

BAILEY: I've been looking for Rosie for over a year. When I saw him the only thing I could think of was getting him back. My mind went blank and I just-I just—

PHIL: Went crazy?

BAILEY: That's what you want me to say, isn't it?

PHIL: You choose the word, I don't care, I just want you to be honest about it.

BAILEY: I went crazy.

PHIL: Okay. I can understand that. We can all go a little crazy once in a while, right?

BAILEY: That's right.

PHIL: I can certainly understand that. See. We just connected. I get you now.

BAILEY: You do?

PHIL: Yes. But that dog is ours.

BAILEY: Now he is.

PHIL: So when you leave here tonight you remember we didn't have to let you do this, you understand? You don't bother us again. Do you understand?

BAILEY: Yes.

PHIL: Good. Then we have an agreement.

BAILEY: When I adopted Rosie I had to put the fees on my credit card because I was completely broke at the time. My grandma died and I had to use my savings to bury her because there wasn't anyone else and her estate was tied up for months. It was just me and her, I won't bore you with the pathetic details but once she died that was it for me as far as blood goes, you know? So I thought to myself, you know what, I'm not going to be depressed, I'm not going to wallow in this, I'm going to start a new life in a new city and I'm going to

adopt something to love. I went to the shelter down off
Goss and they had this like yard thing that you could
take a dog to sort of play with it and see if, I don't
know, see if you're like a match or whatever. And I
had taken three other dogs into the yard with me one
at a time and they didn't care about me, they sniffed
the grass and pooped and peed and waited at the gate
for the attendant to come back. But then I was leaving
and I saw Rosie, I had missed him initially because his
cage was first in this whole huge line of cages and I
guess I just didn't see him, there were so many cages,
one after another for what stretched, I don't know, it
seemed at the time like it went on forever and I just
missed him. But on my way out I spotted him and he
spotted me, we made eye contact and I felt something.
Whatever it was drew me to him and he sat there and
just stared at me and I thought, well hell, one more,
and when we got in the yard he jumped up on me and
licked me and rolled over for me to pet his belly and I
bent down and called him a sweet boy and I rubbed his
belly and he licked my hand and I took out my credit
card and told the attendant "sold!" We both laughed
about that. She told me Rosie had never done that with
anyone else before and I just started crying. Right there
in the yard and Rosie licked my hand and I took him
home and you don't have to understand it, but I had a
bond with him I can't explain.

PHIL: And what if I have that bond with him now?

BAILEY: You don't.

PHIL: Yes I do.

BAILEY: I don't believe you.

PHIL: You don't have to believe me. That dog loves us.
And he keeps us safe. A built in alarm system that dog
is. So you can understand, especially since you have
such similar feelings, our reluctance to just give him

back to you. We love Duke and he's our dog now. We have a very similar story from when we adopted him, you'd be surprised—

BAILEY: I would?

JOAN: *(You're lying)* Phil.

PHIL: You certainly would, you want me to tell it to you? It's just as pretty as your story.

BAILEY: Not really.

PHIL: I love that dog more than you could possibly know.

BAILEY: Okay.

PHIL: You wouldn't want to put us through what you've been through, would you?

BAILEY: No. No I wouldn't. If that were really the case.

PHIL: Tell this woman how much we love that dog—

JOAN: We really do, he's been exactly what we needed after everything—

PHIL: That's enough.

JOAN: Maybe she would understand where *we* were at when we adopted him—

PHIL: No, it's none of her business. Now do me a great big favor and tell this woman how much Duke loves us.

JOAN: He really does. He's a good, good dog.

BAILEY: I know he is. I'm glad to know that he's been so well taken care of all this time. You all are good people for letting me come say goodbye and I appreciate it.

BEN: *(Indicating his empty trifle)* Is there any more of this?

JOAN: No.

BAILEY: I'd like to say goodbye to him now—

JOAN: Of course. He's out back.

PHIL: I'll go with you.

BAILEY: Great. I do really appreciate you letting me do this. I had a dream about Rosie last night and he was walking down this dark alley and he was lost and alone and he was really really scared, somehow I was inside his head and I could read his thoughts and he was really scared that he wasn't going to get where he was going and then he thought of me. He stopped and he thought of me and ran all the way from downtown to my cute little picket fenced house in the suburbs right by the beach, not my real house, the house in my dream, and I was waiting for him on the front porch with his leash and we walked down to the beach and fetched his stick in the waves and we laid out on the beach and watched the sunset. Then I woke up and I felt really good about coming here and doing this. I knew it was what I needed to do. I knew it was the right thing to do. Thank you for having me.

JOAN: It's been no trouble at all.

(BAILEY *stands to go to the backyard. She collects her bag.*)

PHIL: What's with the bag?

BAILEY: I wanted to give him some things, if that's okay?

PHIL: Fine, fine, he'll just tear up whatever it is anyway.

BAILEY: Okay. Well. Here I go.

(BAILEY *exits to the backyard.* PHIL *goes to follow her.*)

PHIL: Be nice to each other, you're the only family you've got. Apologize for being assholes. I'm going to finish this so that I don't have to have that woman in my life anymore.

(PHIL *exits.* JOAN *stands and begins collecting plates and cleaning up.*)

BEN: I just don't need you trying to help me is all, okay?

JOAN: Fine.

BEN: I can take care of myself.

JOAN: I know.

BEN: You make me feel like I'm a kid.

JOAN: Well I don't mean to. You make me feel like an asshole.

BEN: Sometimes you act like an asshole!

JOAN: And sometimes you act like a kid.

BEN: Maybe I do but I don't try and interfere with your life—

JOAN: Bullshit Mr Baseball bat!

BEN: That's different, we were kids.

JOAN: No, it's not.

There is a moment of silence.

BEN: Do you need help?

JOAN: No. I don't.

BEN: Can't you see how embarrassing it is to be set up on a blind date by your sister?

JOAN: I'm so sorry! I don't get it but that's fine!

BEN: You're my big sister!

JOAN: Who cares?

BEN: I care!

JOAN: I'm done talking about this. If you can't understand I'm trying to help you then I'm not going to understand you being embarrassed. She's actually a very nice girl.

BEN: You don't even know her.

JOAN: She's a very nice girl. She's lonely. So are you.

BEN: Give me a break everyone is lonely!

JOAN: That's not true, I don't believe that.

BEN: Believe whatever you want—

JOAN: I'm not a bad person for being concerned about you and I won't let you make me feel like one and that's that. Do you understand?

BEN: No.

JOAN: Fine.

(JOAN *exits to the kitchen with a stack of plates.* BEN *pours himself more wine as* BAILEY *rushes in from the backyard, her duffle bag is now full and appears to be moving and wails a little bit. She sees* BEN. *He smiles at her.*)

BAILEY: I'll blow you if you keep your mouth shut.

BEN: *(Did I hear that right?)* What did you say?

BAILEY: You heard me.

BAILEY rushes out the front door and lets it slam behind her.

BEN: No, no I didn't—

(JOAN *re-enters from the kitchen.*)

JOAN: What was that?

BEN: That was my date.

JOAN: What?

BEN: Bailey just left. I think she was upset.

JOAN: Well that's just not what I would have expected from her after I go to this trouble making the dinner and everything and she can't even say thank you—

BEN: I wouldn't take it personally.

JOAN: It's hard not to.

BEN: Do you have a phone number for her or anything?

JOAN: No, I don't, why, oh what, no, you're not actually, oh god forbid, interested in her are you?

BEN: I don't know.

JOAN: That would make your big bad evil sister actually right about something and that'd just—

(PHIL *rushes in from outside. He is limping.*)

PHIL: *(Catching his breath and limping)* Call…the…police…right now…

JOAN: Phil? What happened?

(PHIL *makes it to the front door and opens it.* BAILEY *is gone.*)

PHIL: Shit. She fucking tazed me with-with some fucking sort of stun gun or something—

JOAN: Tazed you?

PHIL: She's—she's got Duke.

JOAN: What?

PHIL: She—she fucking dog-napped him!

(Blackout)

Scene 4

(A close spotlight on BAILEY*)*

BAILEY: He's my dog! Put me in jail, I don't care, I have rights in this situation, I've done my research, this sort of thing has happened before and there are precedents! I have his paperwork, I can show you…see that's what you don't understand, he was mine first. They adopted him after he was already mine. We have a bond… we're bonded…doesn't that mean anything to you? I was only taking what was mine to begin with. What kind of person keeps someone else's dog? I mean/how would you feel if I just took your child to my house and started acting like it was mine? How would you feel about that? Yeah. That's what I thought. I'm done talking. Are they pressing charges or not?

(*Spotlight out.*)

Scene 5

(*Lights on* BEN *at a police station. He is waiting.* BAILEY *enters from a holding area. She's surprised to see him.*)

BEN: Hi.

BAILEY: Hi.

BEN: How's it going?

BAILEY: I've been better. What are you doing here?

BEN: I thought you might need a ride.

BAILEY: Fuck you.

BEN: I'm sorry?

BAILEY: I said fuck you, I just spent the night in jail because of you—

BEN: Hey, no, wait, not because of me, I didn't have anything to do with it—

BAILEY: I'm not blowing you if that's what you're here for—

BEN: Is that what you said? I had trouble hearing you—

BAILEY: Sure you did.

BEN: I thought you said, "I'm going to take him to my hut."

BAILEY: Oh yeah?

BEN: I swear.

BAILEY: Well that's not what I said, I wanted you to keep your mouth *shut*.

BEN: I did.

BAILEY: A lot of good it did.

BEN: Phil ran in as soon as you left, you should have zapped him harder.

BAILEY: I didn't want to hurt him. Honestly, though, I thought he'd be down longer than that.

BEN: They're both totally pissed at me right now for not stopping you—

BAILEY: They are?

BEN: Yeah.

BAILEY: What would you have done to stop me?

BEN: That's the thing, I didn't want to stop you—

BAILEY: Because you couldn't have stopped me, no one could have stopped me—

BEN: Until the police did.

BAILEY: Yeah.

BEN: I'm sorry.

BAILEY: What do you want?

BEN: I thought that you might need a ride home.

BAILEY: I don't.

BEN: Is there someone here to pick you up?

(BAILEY *is nonplussed.*)

BEN: Well if you need me to I don't mind—

BAILEY: I'd rather walk. I need to be alone. I can't get my car out of impound until Monday thanks to your asshole family. *(She goes to leave.)*

BEN: Can I call you?

BAILEY: What?

BEN: Call you sometime, you know, to like go out and do something or something like that?

BAILEY: Oh yeah right.

BEN: I'm serious.

BAILEY: Why would you want to do that?

BEN: I don't know, I guess I think you're cool—

BAILEY: Oh you do?

BEN: You're a badass. I've never seen anyone do something like that before.

BAILEY: Oh yeah stealing dogs is so fucking cool now I guess.

BEN: Not the dog part, I don't know, taking a stand or more taking back what's yours, fighting the system, the fucking look on Phil's face, it was awesome!

BAILEY: I just want Rosie back.

BEN: Go out with me.

BAILEY: Not a chance. *(She is almost gone.)*

BEN: I have him all next week.

BAILEY: What did you say?

BEN: You heard me. Duke, or Rosie, I have him, or I mean I'm dog sitting while Joan and Phil are on a cruise.

BAILEY: I hope the ship is invaded by pirates—

BEN: I don't think that happens—

BAILEY: Then I hope it like dies and there's shit floating in the pool and sloshing down the hall. I know that happens because I saw it on the news.

BEN: Yeah, that could happen.

BAILEY: And you're watching Rosie?

BEN: I'm staying at their house all week. We could do something if you wanted?

BAILEY: We could?

BEN: I usually just take him to the park, let him run the dog park, you know the one that's in Cherokee?

BAILEY: I know it.

BEN: You can't do anything crazy, though, I mean it, they'd kill me.

BAILEY: The cops told me Phil would press charges next time I tried to take him. I can't go to jail, I mean honestly, seriously, I am not this person. I've never stolen anything but a pack of Wrigley's from the gas station when I was five. I know you think that I'm crazy, but I'm not. He just started going on and on about how much he loved Rosie and I just couldn't take it. Was he lying?

BEN: I couldn't say.

BAILEY: Does he love him like he was talking about?

BEN: It's more Joan's dog. She's the one that wanted to get it after he cheated on her.

BAILEY: Ah-ha! I knew there was something with them. He's such an asshole.

BEN: He made a mistake.

BAILEY: You haven't answered my question—

BEN: Which was what?

BAILEY: Was he lying?

BEN: He was a little high—

BAILEY: I'm not crazy, okay?

BEN: I don't think you're crazy, why would I want to hang out with you?

BAILEY: Maybe you like crazy.

BEN: Maybe just a little bit.

BAILEY: So was he lying or not? Just answer me—

BEN: He was lying. He didn't even adopt him, Joan did.

BAILEY: That asshole! God, he's good isn't he? What does he do?

BEN: Something with the stock market. I don't really know.

BAILEY: Thank you for telling me that.

BEN: You're welcome.

BAILEY: So you want to meet at the park or what?

BEN: Sure, that'd be great. They leave Monday morning and I'm going to be staying at their house so—

BAILEY: Great, Monday afternoon then?

BEN: Sure.

BAILEY: I'm off at five.

BEN: Where do you work?

BAILEY: I'm not telling you. I can be at the park by 5:15.

BEN: Great, sounds great, we'll be there. Are you sure you don't want a ride?

BAILEY: I'm sure. Thank you though, for, you know, letting me run out with my dog in a duffle bag.

BEN: Don't mention it. I'll see you Monday.

BAILEY: Okay. No blow jobs though.

BEN: Fine.

BAILEY: I can't wait to see Rosie again.

(Lights fade to black as BAILEY *exits. The sound of a dog howling is heard in the black.)*

Scene 6

(A dog park. BEN *stands at a fence.* BAILEY *enters and she walks to him.)*

BAILEY: Hey.

BEN: Hey, you made it.

BAILEY: Sorry I'm a little late.

BEN: It's fine, no big deal. Duke's playing—

BAILEY: *(Calling)* Rosie! Rosie!

(The unseen dog runs over to the fence. BAILEY *reaches over it.)*

BAILEY: Hi baby! Are you having fun? You are my sweetie-boy! Go get 'em!

(The unseen dog runs off to play.)

BEN: He loves you.

BAILEY: No shit.

(There is a moment of silence.)

BEN: Duke was a big part—

BAILEY: Hey, can we just call him Rosie when I'm around? You can call him Duke as soon as I'm gone but for me, that's not his name.

BEN: Sure. I understand.

BAILEY: No you don't.

BEN: Okay.

BAILEY: What the hell am I doing here?

BEN: Going on a date?

BAILEY: That's not what this is.

BEN: Why not?

BAILEY: What do you mean why not?

BEN: Do you think I'm ugly?

BAILEY: I never said that.

BEN: Do you think I'm gross because I only have one ball?

BAILEY: Of course not.

BEN: Duke...um I mean...Rosie was a big help to me when I was recovering, I stayed with Joan right after the operation and he would sleep with me every night and lick my cheek in the morning to wake me up.

BAILEY: He did that?

BEN: Yup.

BAILEY: I love knowing that.

BEN: He was amazing.

BAILEY: He is amazing.

BEN: I know. I do understand why you would want to get him back. He's special.

BAILEY: He is special. Thank you for saying that. We took a trip together once, I just wanted to get out of town and be in nature so I took him up to Nolin Lake and we got one of those little cabins, have you ever been there?

BEN: Not since I was a kid—

BAILEY: It still looks exactly the same. Nothing's changed. We had our own cabin and at night I wanted to go out on a hike and there are all those trails and everything you know, and some of them are marked better than others but my flashlight died. We were out almost two miles I think and I started to freak out because the moon was pretty bright, I mean, I could see the trail mostly but I got all turned around and couldn't find any markers and so I just sort of sat down, to breathe and get my bearings and Rosie just

started licking my cheek and pulling me on the leash
down a certain path. I decided what the hell right?
I might as well let him try and sure as shit enough
we were back at our cabin and he ran up to the door
and jumped up and wagged his tail and I just, I don't
know. I've never loved anything more than I loved him
in that moment. He made me feel like a human being
and I changed that night.

BEN: How so?

BAILEY: I stopped trying to lead life so much and
started— *(She pauses.)* —I started following my guides.

BEN: Your guides, huh?

BAILEY: Don't look at me like I'm being hoaky
or something, whatever you want to call it, your
intuition—

BEN: My sister's tried talking to me about this stuff
before, I don't think it's my thing.

BAILEY: It doesn't matter. It's how the universe works
and you gotta let go and follow it sometimes. That's
what Rosie taught me. That's why he's so special to
me.

BEN: I mean, it's a great story, I totally get it, I'm not
downing you or anything.

BAILEY: Phil doesn't have a story like that. Neither does
Joan.

BEN: Yeah. I don't know. I mean, I feel for you but I
don't know what to say about it, you know?

BAILEY: It's okay.

BEN: I wonder if this has happened to anyone before.

BAILEY: Oh yeah, I found some stories online and
they ended with the new owners giving the dog back
on their own, you know, because they ultimately

understood and they couldn't keep the dogs, they just couldn't, because it wasn't the right thing to do.

BEN: Oh.

BAILEY: So that's where I'm at.

BEN: Maybe you shouldn't have pushed her into the pond.

BAILEY: I should have pushed him! That asshole… he would've never given me my dog back, even if I'd have walked up to them calmly and stated my case he would have laughed at me and walked away.

BEN: Maybe, but now you'll never know.

BAILEY: But at least the way it did go down: he didn't laugh.

(There is a moment of awkward silence.)

BEN: I don't know what else to say about it.

BAILEY: I know.

(Beat)

BEN: So what else do you like besides dogs?

BAILEY: What do you mean?

BEN: I mean, you know, what else do you do, for fun or whatever?

BAILEY: Do you want to fuck me?

BEN: What?

BAILEY: Do you?

BEN: Yeah.

BAILEY: Right now?

BEN: At the park?

BAILEY: Your place.

BEN: Joan and Phil's place is closer, it's where I'm staying all week.

BAILEY: Fine. You wanna go?

BEN: Sure. Okay.

BAILEY: I need to shower first but after that we could just have sex and it would be the easiest thing, don't you think?

BEN: *(Calling out)* Rosie!

(Lights fade to black. A dog panting is heard in the dark.)

Scene 7

(Darkness. We hear BEN and BAILEY having sex [doggy style] over the couch at JOAN and PHIL's. It's rough and wild and they're both having the time of their lives. They climax. BEN sighs, satisfied, and BAILEY laughs. It starts small but becomes almost maniacal. He rises and puts on some shorts and turns the lights on. She wraps a blanket that was hung over the couch around her shoulders and collapses down onto it.)

BEN: What's so funny?

BAILEY: That was amazing.

BEN: So why's it so funny?

BAILEY: It's not, I'm sorry, it wasn't funny, it was incredible.

BEN: I just don't get why you're laughing.

BAILEY: *(Through laughter)* I'm sorry.

BEN: Stop!

BAILEY: I'm sorry!

BEN: What's so funny?!?

BAILEY: That was the first time I've sex in over a year.

BEN: Longer for me.

BAILEY: It's pretty pathetic, isn't it?

BEN: Yeah, I guess.

BAILEY: When was yours?

BEN: Before the surgery. My ex, she was the last person I was with.

(BAILEY *laughs again.*)

BEN: That funny too?

BAILEY: I'm sorry. It's this whole thing. I'm just…like I'm just totally overcome with how funny life is, you know? I mean it's so funny!

BEN: I was more thinking hot as hell, but I guess we all see things differently.

BAILEY: No, I mean, yes, hot as hell, that would be the only justifiable way to describe the sex we just had but I mean, here I am. With you. I can't help it. It's funny. Think about it.

Ben: *(Snickering)* I guess you're right.

BAILEY: I pushed your sister into a pond.

BEN: *(Mimicking)* My watch!

BAILEY: I tazed your brother in law.

BEN: *(Mimicking)* She-she fucking dog-napped him!

BAILEY: Shut up he did not say that!

BEN: Honest to god.

BAILEY: What would your sister say if she saw us right now?

BEN: She'd freak out. "You did it on my couch!"

BAILEY: Over, it was over the couch!

BEN: Yeah, sis, not a seed spilled and totally protected.

(BAILEY *and* BEN *both are hysterical.*)

BAILEY: See, that's funny!

BEN: You're right.

BAILEY: Yay for same planes! It took you long enough!

BEN: Come on, I'm slow.

(BAILEY *and* BEN *laugh. He lights a joint.*)

BEN: You want?

BAILEY: I guess. Just a little. So you smoke, like every day?

BEN: Sometimes.

BAILEY: Sometimes?

BEN: Like some days.

BAILEY: I mean it doesn't bother me, you don't do any other drugs do you?

BEN: Pot isn't a drug.

BAILEY: That's so stupid. Coffee is a drug.

BEN: Good point. No. Just pot.

BAILEY: I mean I really don't care.

BEN: Then yes. Every day.

BAILEY: I guess since the surgery especially?

BEN: Pretty much since I got out of high school. Some people take Prozac, I smoke pot.

BAILEY: I take Prozac.

(BEN *stares at* BAILEY *for a moment not sure what to say.*)

BAILEY: I'm kidding! I'm not on Prozac…

BEN: I'm not judging or anything.

BAILEY: I take Xanax when I need it, but mostly just since Rosie, you know.

BEN: Yeah.

(BAILEY *and* BEN *pause, not uncomfortably, but one of those completely comfortable pauses that lets you know you're connecting with someone.*)

BEN: So what do you want to do?

BAILEY: I guess get something to eat?

BEN: No, I mean, like what do you want to do with your life. I don't know anything about you.

BAILEY: I know. That's how I like it.

BEN: Come on. Give me something. One fact. One little nugget.

BAILEY: I work at a shelter.

BEN: No shit, really?

BAILEY: It's my shelter, actually, I started it. Once my grandmother's estate settled I had a large chunk of cash and I turned this old pet store into a no-kill shelter.

BEN: No shit?

BAILEY: No shit.

BEN: Wow. How long have you had it?

BAILEY: It just opened last month. I wasn't sleeping those first few weeks after Rosie got out and I was lying in bed at like four in the morning crying and it just sort of came to me. I thought that it was something I could do. So I did it.

BEN: You thought you'd find him if you had your own shelter?

BAILEY: I had thought that would be neat, you know, like the kind of thing that would happen in the movie version of my life. Then the money from the estate came through a couple of weeks after I lost Rosie and it all just kind of aligned perfectly.

BEN: And you love it?

BAILEY: I love it.

BEN: That's cool.

BAILEY: Yeah.

(Another one of those nice pauses)

BAILEY: Okay, go, give me one nugget too, it's not fair if it's just me.

BEN: Oh, okay. Yeah, so I draw comic books.

BAILEY: Anything I would've seen? Like Batman or something?

BEN: I've been writing my own. I'm trying to pitch it to different publishers right now, trying to get my name out there, you know? I actually have a meeting to show off some of my stuff later this week, so we'll see.

BAILEY: That's great. I can't smoke anymore of that.

BEN: That's cool.

BEN puts the joint out on his tongue and swallows what's left of it.

BAILEY: Oh my god what are you doing?

BEN: What? I ate it.

BAILEY: Do people do that?

BEN: I do.

BAILEY: Well okay then.

BEN: So can I ask you a sort of obvious question?

BAILEY: No new nuggets, not yet.

BEN: This is about the nugget I already know about.

BAILEY: Fine. What?

BEN: If you have your own shelter, you have animals there, right?

BAILEY: Of course, that's what a shelter is.

BEN: How many?

BAILEY: It changes, right now I have seventeen dogs and twenty-nine cats.

BEN: So what's wrong with them?

BAILEY: Nothings wrong with them, they're all healthy, my shelter is really clean, the units are all brand new and—

BEN: I mean what's wrong with one of them for you? Why don't you adopt one of them?

BAILEY: Oh, okay, I see what you're getting at now. *(She gets up and begins retrieving her clothes and dressing.)*

BEN: What, what are you doing?

BAILEY: It's getting late.

BEN: I thought we were going to eat.

BAILEY: I gotta go.

BEN: Are you upset with me?

BAILEY: No.

BEN: Yes you are, what, what's the matter?

BAILEY: Nothing.

BEN: Because I asked you about getting another animal, what's the big deal?

BAILEY: You don't get it, alright, I can't explain it.

BEN: Don't go.

BAILEY: I really need to. I'm sorry.

BEN: What about tomorrow, you want to meet at the park again?

BAILEY: I don't know.

BEN: Come on, why not, I have Rosie all week, might as well take advantage of it, right?

BAILEY: Are you sure that's alright with you?

BEN: I wouldn't ask if it wasn't. I'm sorry if I upset you.

BAILEY: I just get sad, that's all.

BEN: Let me make it up to you. I can make us a picnic. We could see Shakespeare in the Park tomorrow night, they let dogs on the grassy part.

BAILEY: I know. We've been.

BEN: You want to go with us, tomorrow night?

BAILEY: Okay. I'll bring some treats for Rosie I know he likes. There's a dog bakery over by the shelter and they make all kinds of little goodies, he loves peanut butter.

BEN: That sounds great. I'll meet you at the dog park at five-fifteen.

(BAILEY *goes to the back door.*)

BAILEY: *(Off)* Mommy's gonna go now but I'll see you tomorrow, okay my sweet boy, okay? *(She re-enters and grabs her bag.)*

BEN: Five-fifteen?

BAILEY: I'm actually off tomorrow, my days off are Tuesdays and Wednesdays, that's when I have the most volunteers, so I just check in first thing and that's it.

BEN: Yeah?

BAILEY: So I could meet you earlier, if you want?

BEN: I want.

BAILEY: Okay. I'll meet you at the dog park at eight A M.

BEN: Oh. Okay. Eight A M?

BAILEY: Is that too early?

BEN: It's kinda early—

BAILEY: I thought maybe you'd let me chip Rosie—

BEN: Chip her, what do you mean?

BAILEY: You can insert a microchip into a dog and then you can find them if you get separated.

BEN: I don't know.

BAILEY: I'll pay for it, I'm sure Phil and Joan won't mind, it'll give them piece of mind if anything. I should have done it back when he was mine but I didn't know about it, a lot of people don't even think about it, like I'm sure Phil hasn't, you know?

BEN: Well, is it very invasive?

BAILEY: Oh no, we'll still be able to catch Shakespeare and have a picnic and all of that stuff. That's why so early, it'll give us plenty of time.

BEN: Okay then, I guess that'll be okay.

BAILEY: Are you going to kiss me goodbye or what?

(BEN *jumps up and kisses* BAILEY, *she lets him linger for a moment. Lights fade to black. The sound of several dogs barking and fighting is heard in the dark.*)

Scene 8

(BAILEY *and* BEN *are lounging and cuddling in their pajamas on the couch at* JOAN *and* PHIL'*s place.* BEN *begins to playfully nudge* BAILEY *with his head and whining like a dog wanting a treat.*)

BAILEY: Stop it.

BEN: Stop what?

BAILEY: Stop shifting your weight, it's messing with my center of gravity.

BEN: Sorry.

BAILEY: There. That's perfect. Stay there.

(BEN *does his best "am I a good boy" pose with his tongue out and his paws up, if he had a tail it would be wagging.*)

BAILEY: *(Petting his head)* That's a good boy.

BEN: I am a good boy.

BAILEY: We'll see.

BEN: They'll be home this weekend.

BAILEY: I know. Shut up.

BEN: Sorry.

BAILEY: I don't want to talk about them.

BEN: We don't have to, it's just we're going to have to do this at your place from now on instead of—

BAILEY: I know alright.

BEN: You okay.

BAILEY: I'm fine. It'll be great.

BEN: Good.

(BAILEY *and* BEN *kiss.*)

BAILEY: And you can just bring Rosie over to my place instead of the park when you—

BEN: I don't have the dog when they're in town, it's their dog—

BAILEY: But you said you were close—

BEN: We are—

BAILEY: You said when you were sick he laid with you—

BEN: He did but I was staying here while I was recuperating.

BAILEY: Oh.

BEN: I don't just like take him when they're in town, that'd be weird, wouldn't it?

BAILEY: Why would that be weird?

BEN: It's their dog.

BAILEY: I just thought you were close, that's all, that's all I was thinking, that you maybe came over while they were at work or something like that and took him for a walk just to get him out, don't you ever do that?

BEN: I have stuff going on.

BAILEY: Well, you're on disability right now so I didn't know—

BEN: What are you talking about?

BAILEY: What? What do you mean?

BEN: I'm doing stuff and I told you all about it!

BAILEY: I know you are, it's just not like it's taking all day, I mean right now, I was talking about right now, not once you found something.

BEN: Okay.

BAILEY: Okay.

BEN: Are you mad because I won't have Duke with me the next time we hang out?

BAILEY: Rosie.

BEN: Are you?

BAILEY: I'm not mad.

BEN: What's the matter, you just totally iced up—

BAILEY: You're the one who brought up your sister and her lovely husband.

BEN: I thought we should at least like, have the conversation?

BAILEY: Is that what you want to go ahead and do?

BEN: What?

BAILEY: Go ahead and have this conversation?

BEN: I just wanted to remind you—

BAILEY: No, let's have the conversation that we really should be having right now.

BEN: And what conversation is that?

BAILEY: The conversation where I tell you that there is no us without Rosie. If Rosie isn't going to be around then I'm not going to be around. I thought you understood that, I'm sorry, I didn't write it down and give it to you or anything, but just so you know, there is no such thing as you and I when you don't have my dog on your arm, okay?

BEN: Are you serious right now?

BAILEY: Dead serious.

BEN: That's fucked up.

BAILEY: No more fucked up than you!

BEN: What are you talking about, we were just laying here having a nice time and—

BAILEY: And you wanted to have this conversation!

BEN: No I didn't! This is just so fucked up that you'd say that to me.

BAILEY: Oh get off of it! Look at you, what you were doing!

BEN: What? What was I doing?

BAILEY: Preying on some heartbroken woman for some pussy and using her dog as dick bait!

BEN: That's not what was going on here and you know it.

BAILEY: You're a hypocrite, that's what I know!

BEN: And you're a bitch!

BAILEY: Yes, yes, call me a bitch, please, that's what you do when a woman does something you don't like you call them a bitch so do it, go on, DO IT!

BEN: Bitch!

BAILEY barks at him, growls and looks as if she might attack him.

BEN: Get away from me; you're crazy! Get out of here!

BAILEY: *(Growling)* I'm not crazy and I'm not going anywhere, we're going to talk.

BEN: Stop barking at me and *acting* crazy or get out, you understand? What's the matter with you?

BAILEY: I thought you wanted me to be a bitch.

BEN: I don't, alright. I don't want that. Let's just—fuck why did you say that to me!

BAILEY: I don't know. You scare me.

BEN: I scare you?

BAILEY: Yeah.

BEN: Did you mean it?

BAILEY: Can we stop acting like assholes, please? I mean what the hell just happened, we were sitting here and having a nice time—

BEN: I'll tell you what happened you told me you were basically using me to be around your dog.

BAILEY: That's correct. And we clarified what you were doing with me too, didn't we?

BEN: We didn't clarify anything-I like you!

BAILEY: You might now but not at first.

BEN: Always!

BAILEY: And what about the blowjob?

BEN: I thought you said something else!

BAILEY: You knew what I said. You knew I told you I'd give you a blowjob even after I already knew you only had one ball and that's why you came to pick me up.

BEN: It's not true, you're—

BAILEY: If you call me crazy one more time you're really going to see crazy. That's not fair.

(BEN *stares at* BAILEY *unsure of what to say.*)

BAILEY: Just admit it. We can cancel shit out. Just admit you used my dog to get me in bed. We can forget the entire last seven minutes if you just admit to it even for just a smidgen, we can forget—

BEN: We can?

BAILEY: Yes.

BEN: Fine, Okay, yes. Maybe part of me thought because I was going to be watching the dog, that maybe you'd want to, just hang out, nothing sexual, that you'd at least want to hang out. Alright.

BAILEY: Nothing sexual? That's bullshit.

BEN: I mean, I hoped, of course I hoped, I'm a guy!

BAILEY: Great. Thank you.

BEN: And what about you.

BAILEY: I saw an opportunity to see my dog and I did think you were cute—

BEN: You did?

BAILEY: I did.

BEN: And now?

BAILEY: Now I still do and you're fun.

BEN: I think that you're fun too.

BAILEY: I also, though, if we're being honest, hate thinking about Rosie being here all day by himself and since I have Tuesdays and Wednesdays totally off and since your schedule, is like, you know, really flexible right now, I was just thinking, you know? Maybe we could just take him out a couple times, if there's nothing else going on. That's all I was thinking.

BEN: It'd be weird, what if they found out?

BAILEY: Be honest with them. Tell them you missed him.

BEN: I guess I could.

BAILEY: They'd probably be grateful.

BEN: I don't see why it'd be such a big deal.

BAILEY: I don't either.

BEN: Okay. If I'm not working. I can pick him up.

(BAILEY *throws her arms around* BEN.)

BAILEY: I'm starting to love you, you know? Did you know that?

BEN: Really?

BAILEY: Yes. What about you?

BEN: Me too.

(BAILEY *and* BEN *begin passionately making out as pajamas begin to loosen. There is the sound of a car door slamming shut. Another one*)

BAILEY: Did you hear that?

BEN: Hear what?

JOAN: *(Off/screaming)* I need your key Phil!

BEN: Oh Christ. They're home already.

BAILEY: Oh Christ.

BEN: Hurry, back here/

(BAILEY *and* BEN *quickly begin gathering clothing and blankets and exit to the bedroom. We hear the sound of a door unlocking as* PHIL *and* JOAN *enter,* PHIL *carrying the luggage. He drops it all in a pile once the door is shut.*)

PHIL: What's that smell?

JOAN: Get the rest of your stuff and get out.

PHIL: I want to talk.

JOAN: I want to cut your cock off and feed it to the dog.

PHIL: It didn't mean anything!

JOAN: Oh yes it did.

PHIL: It was an innocent/she needed help with her buckle—

JOAN: What's wrong with me?

PHIL: Nothing is wrong with you.

JOAN: Then there must be something wrong with you.

PHIL: Let's call that shrink again…maybe you're right…maybe I do need/

JOAN: No. Not again. Pack, I want you out, right now.

PHIL: What if I just slept on the couch?

JOAN: Where are my scissors anyway?

PHIL: Ok.ay

(PHIL *exits to the bedroom.* JOAN *starts to ugly cry.*)

PHIL: *(Off)* What the hell are you doing here?

(BAILEY *and* BEN *exit the bedroom followed by* PHIL.)

BAILEY & BEN: Hi.

JOAN: Ben? What is this?

BEN: This is Bailey.

PHIL: We know who it is, what are you doing?

JOAN: Phil, I'll handle this—

PHIL: Fine, handle it!

JOAN: You don't tell me what to do EVER AGAIN!

PHIL: I'm sorry.

JOAN: Ben, really? What's going on?

BEN: Why are you home early? What's going on with you? Are you alright?

JOAN: I asked you first!

BEN: We were just hanging out.

BAILEY: Everything is fine, Rosie is fine-I mean Duke, he's been a good boy. And look, they dropped off your watch the other day.

JOAN: They did?

BAILEY: It's over there on the table. It's a beautiful watch. I didn't want to open it but the guy who delivered it insisted to confirm that it was working.

PHIL: That was very diligent of him.

BAILEY: No wonder it costs six hundred dollars when you get service like that, right Phil?

JOAN: I want to see it.

PHIL: You can look at your watch later, I wanna know what the hell—

JOAN: I WANT TO SEE MY WATCH RIGHT NOW!

(*Everyone freezes.* JOAN *goes to the watch and opens the box. She examines it. She smiles and then holds back a tear. She takes it from the box and hurls it at* PHIL *and it hits him, preferably in the crotch.*)

PHIL: Hey!

JOAN: There's your precious watch back!

PHIL: You're going to break it again!

JOAN: Bill me!

PHIL: That hurt!

JOAN: So does this!

(*They all stare at each other for several moments. The pause is as uncomfortable as a tooth extraction.*)

PHIL: Where's Duke?

BAILEY: He's in the backyard.

PHIL: He better be. I want to see my dog.

JOAN: He's my dog, he's always been my dog.

(PHIL *runs out to the backyard.*)

BEN: What's going on?

JOAN: Ben, please answer my question, what is she doing here?

BEN: We've been, well we've been—

BAILEY: Fucking. We've been fucking.

JOAN: Here?

BEN: No!

BAILEY: Not mostly—

JOAN: I—

BEN: What's the matter with you? Why are you home early? What the hell was all of that?

JOAN: He couldn't keep his hands to himself for five days and he was- I mean we weren't even there for twenty-four hours! Twenty-four hours! Oh I don't want to talk about it with you, I want you to leave, both of you—

BEN: I'm going to kill him—

JOAN: No, no you're not, I'm going to kill him as soon as the two of you get the hell out of my house.

BEN: Joan—

JOAN: I'm serious.

BEN: But look, look at her and I, see you were right, though, don't you see, I do really like her, you knew when you set us up—

JOAN: IT WASN'T A SET-UP I NEEDED EVEN NUMBERS!

(PHIL *enters from the backyard.*)

PHIL: Where is he? What've you done with him?

BAILEY: What are you talking about, he's back there—

PHIL: No, no he isn't. Where is he?

BAILEY: He was out there— (*She runs out to the backyard.*)

PHIL: If you gave her our Duke, Ben, I swear to Christ—

BEN: I didn't do anything! You better back off me you fucking dog!

PHIL: (*To* JOAN) You told him?

BEN: He was in the backyard just a few minutes ago.

PHIL: Then where is he now?

BEN: How should I know?

JOAN: If he says he didn't do anything then he didn't, stop interrogating him.

PHIL: If he didn't do anything then where's Duke?

(BAILEY *re-enters.*)

BAILEY: He's-he's gone-he isn't back there—

PHIL: What did you do?

BAILEY: I didn't do anything, he's gone again. He got out of the yard. The fence in the back looks like it's been pulled down.

JOAN: (*To* PHIL) I told you to fix that, didn't I?

PHIL: Yes.

JOAN: Well there then that's what you get. Your precious Duke off to find his next great love!

PHIL: She did this.

JOAN: No, I don't think so.

PHIL: She did, you can tell by that smug look on her face. She—

JOAN: NO, I DON'T THINK SO. Must've seen a squirrel or something. Don't you think?

BAILEY: He must've.

JOAN: He loves going for squirrels.

BAILEY: Rosie goes for what he wants.

JOAN: I hope he gets it.

BAILEY: Me too.

PHIL: I'm calling the police. *(He takes out his phone and dials.)*

JOAN: No. No police. No distractions. He got out. That's it. I want you to pack the rest of your crap. Forget the dog, it's the least of your worries right now. I'm calling the shots right now, you got it? Hang up or so help me I will gut you like a pig.

(PHIL hangs up the phone.)

PHIL: Fine.

JOAN: Thank you. Go. Pack.

(PHIL exits to the bedroom.)

JOAN: I think that I want the two of you to get dressed and leave.

BAILEY: We're leaving. I'm sorry—

JOAN: It's fine. Really.

BAILEY: I can't speak for Rosie, but I know he was happy. Being with you did make him happy. He loved you.

JOAN: Thank you for saying that. I want to get a new dog now, is that terrible? How soon is too soon?

BAILEY: Everyone's different. There's so much love out there that no one even wants, it just needs to be picked up by anyone who will take it. Anyone who needs it.

JOAN: I might need it soon.

BAILEY: I know a place.

JOAN: Can we go right now? Is it too late?

BAILEY: If you want to. I have the key.

JOAN: Something small though, maybe I could put it in a bag and keep it with me. So that I don't lose it.

BAILEY: Sometimes things come back.

JOAN: Only if they're meant to, people don't just say that because it sounds nice, it's true. And I'm glad.

BAILEY: Thank you. You really want to go right now?

JOAN: Absolutely. But should we have a glass of wine before we go?

BAILEY & BEN: Yes.

JOAN: Phil! Phil! Get some wine! I'm thirsty and so are our guests! Phil do it right now! Phil!

(PHIL *enters from the bedroom and walks into the kitchen with his tail between his legs.* JOAN *begins laughing like a crazy person. We hear a glass break in the kitchen.*)

JOAN: Jesus, Phil, what are you doing?

(JOAN *exits to the kitchen.* BEN *smiles at* BAILEY.)

BEN: Do you have Rosie?

BAILEY: I might know who does.

BEN: You're a badass.

BAILEY: I know.

BEN: I like you. Like a lot.

(BAILEY *smiles at* BEN.)

BAILEY: I like you too.

(JOAN *re-enters carrying a bottle of wine and three glasses. She hands them both a glass and pours as* PHIL *exits from the kitchen with his own glass. He approaches them and* JOAN *growls slightly and bears her teeth.*)

JOAN: Back to packing.

PHIL: Yes dear.

(JOAN *laughs as* PHIL *turns to exit. The three of them toast their glasses as lights fade slowly to black.*)

END OF PLAY

www.ingramcontent.com/pod-product-compliance
Lightning Source LLC
Chambersburg PA
CBHW070026110426
42741CB00034B/2619